The Most Special Gift

Explaining Organ Donation to Children

Acknowledgements:

We want to thank Mid-America Transplant for a partnership grant with Lost & Found Grief Center that provided the funding and impetus for writing this book. We are grateful to Mid-America Transplant staff members, Merry Smith and Julia Brunner, for their careful review of the work to ensure accuracy as we broached this difficult but important explanation for children.

We are grateful to Lost & Found volunteer, Lindsey Novak for her editing contributions and to Meagan Ivey for her wonderful illustrations.

Most importantly, we are grateful to all donors and families who make the important decision to become organ donors, providing the special gift of life to others in the face of a tragedy.

Lost & Found
grief center

Mid·America
TRANSPLANT
FOUNDATION

Dear Caregiver,

Explaining the concept of organ donation to a child is a process that unfolds over time. We wrote this book to help you start the conversation. Below are further ideas to help you as you begin this journey.

- Gather resources: Before talking about organ donation, it is generally best to talk with your child about the concept of death. Many children's books are available at local libraries or bookstores. Other resources are available on the internet.

- Follow your child's lead: Answer the questions your child asks as honestly and simply as you can. Don't be afraid to say "I don't know." Children typically process information in small chunks. It is normal for children to ask the same questions repeatedly as they try to make sense of this topic.

- Affirm emotions: Assure your child that it is okay to feel any emotion.

- Create a safe place for expressing emotions: You might want to designate a specific place in the house where your child can go during times of intense emotion. You can provide items such as a pillow your child can punch, paper and crayons for drawing, a CD of calming music, etc.

- Designate a resource person: Ask an adult whom your child trusts to serve as a resource person. Children often don't want to burden their caregiver by asking questions. Let your child know this adult is available to listen, and answer any questions he or she may have.

- Allow time for free play: Children process the world through playing. Your child may incorporate themes of death or organ donation into his or her playtime.

- Seek professional help when needed: Don't hesitate to speak with your child's school counselor or seek other professional help if you are in any way concerned about your child.

- Take good care of yourself: Remember to take time out when possible for your own self-care. Children often take their cues from the adults around them, and the better you are able to cope, the more likely it is that your child will also cope well.

Sincerely,

Dr. Karen Scott
Sarah Brown

Julian sat on his couch, hugging his favorite teddy bear, Boo, because he was feeling very sad. Something bad had happened to his daddy. His mom and all the other adults were very sad. They were talking softly and crying. Julian was very scared.

As Julian sat, he thought about his visit to the hospital yesterday to see his daddy who was hurt very badly in an accident.

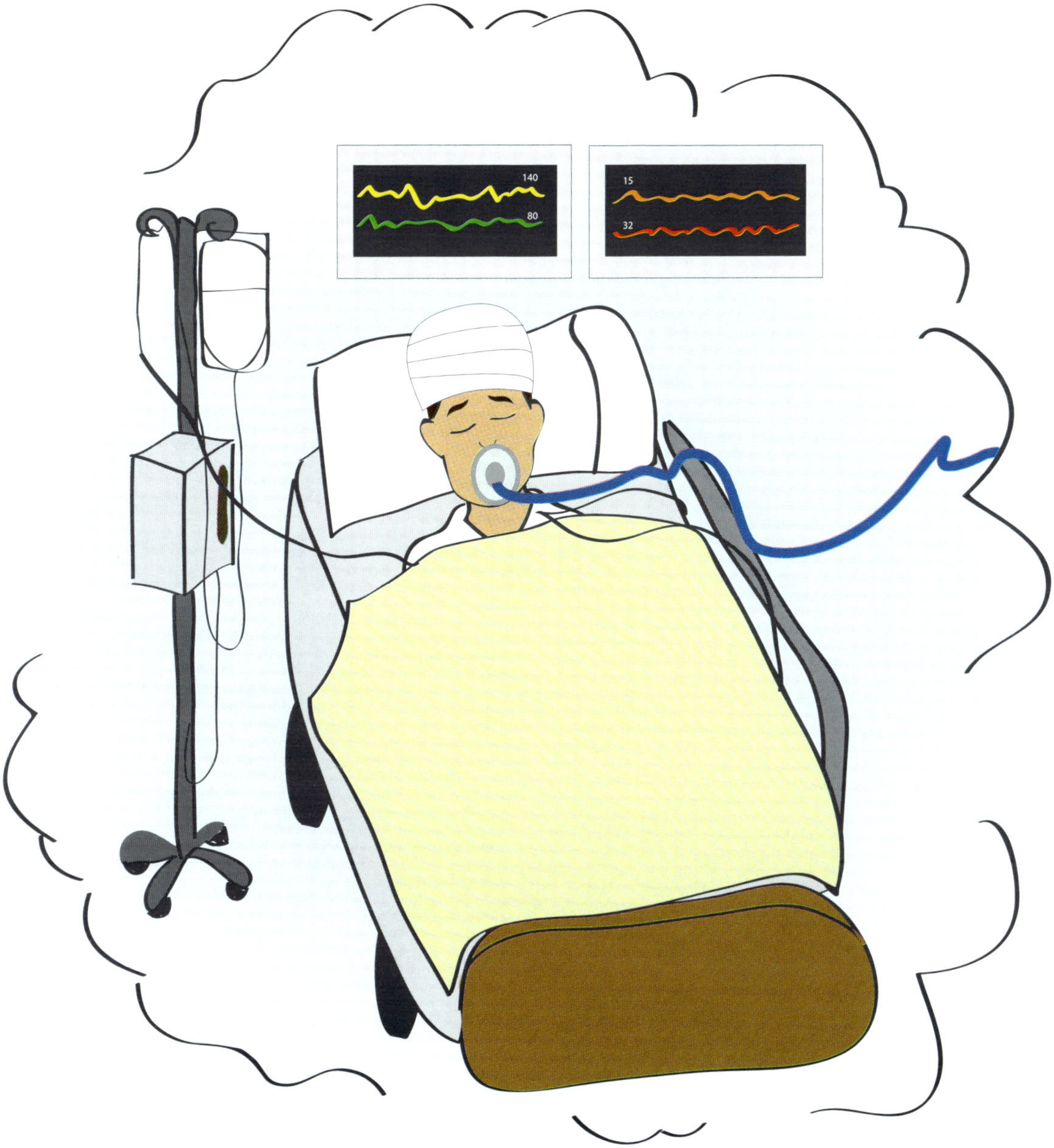

He couldn't stop thinking about how his daddy looked.

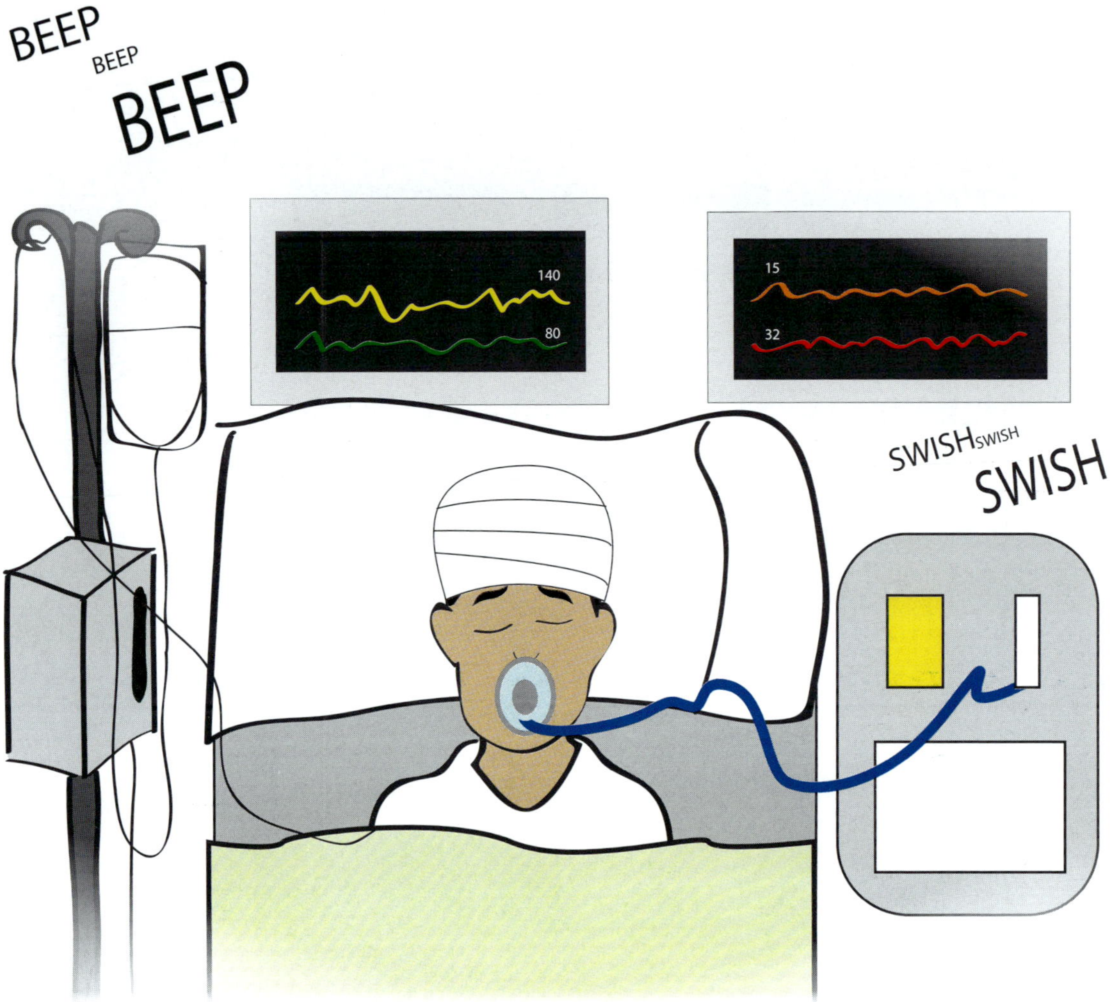

His daddy was in a hospital bed, and it didn't even look like him.

There were lots of tubes in his body and machines around him that made odd sounds. There was beeping, swishing, and all kinds of strange noises coming from the machines.

His daddy couldn't see him and couldn't talk. Julian was very upset and confused.

After a few minutes, Julian's Aunt Mary took him back home.

When Julian got home, he tried to play, but he didn't feel like it.

Aunt Mary tried to get him to eat, but he didn't feel hungry. She even offered his favorite ice cream, but he just didn't want it. He was too worried about his daddy.

After a long night without much sleep, Julian was waiting for his mother to come home from the hospital, holding Boo like he always did when he needed comfort.

Julian's mom came over to the couch and put her arms around him and hugged him tightly. He was very scared and sad because his mom looked so sad.

She said, "Julian, I am very sorry, but your daddy died. The doctors did everything they could but he was hurt so badly in the accident that they couldn't save him."

Julian and his mom cried together.

DONATE

"We are very sad, and we will miss your daddy so much," Julian's mom told him. "He was a very special man and always helped other people."

"I want to tell you about a special decision we made. Sometimes when people die, parts of their bodies can be used to help other people who are very sick. This is called organ donation."

“What does that mean?” Julian asked in confusion.

"The doctors looked at your daddy's brain with special equipment that showed them his brain was not working. It was not sending signals to the rest of his body to make the other parts work," explained his mom.

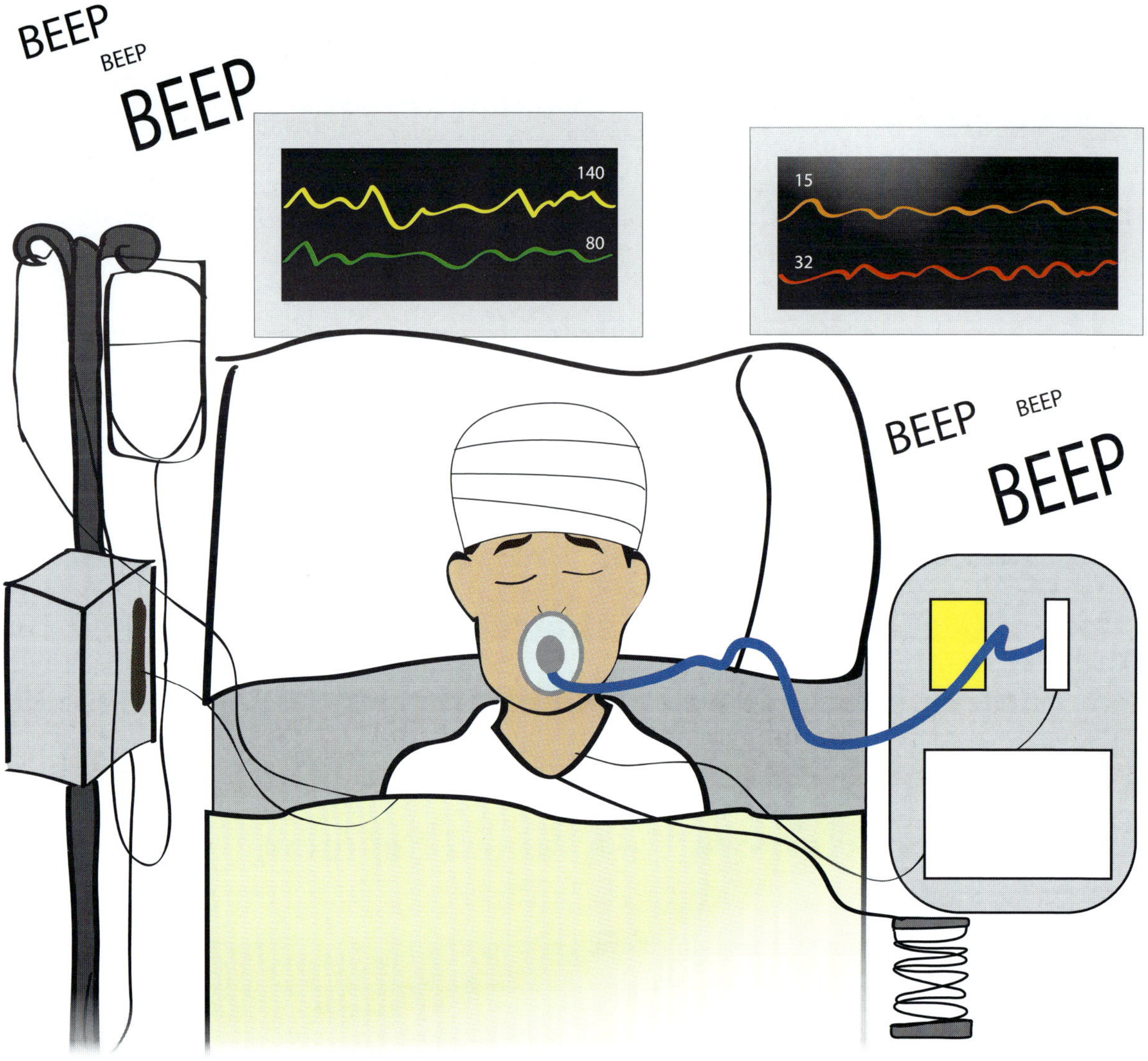

"His brain was hurt so badly, the doctors couldn't fix it. Your dad couldn't feel anything, or see anything, or talk, or think. He didn't even hurt."

"Are you sure?" Julian asked.

"Yes," his mom said. "The doctors checked your daddy's brain and body over and over to be sure."

"Remember the machines you saw? They were doing the work for his brain. They were making his heart pump, and his lungs breathe, but they couldn't keep doing that forever."

"But what is organ donation?

What is an organ?"
Julian asked.

“**Organ donation** is a very special gift that helps other people. **Organs** are parts of the body, like the heart, lungs, and kidneys.”

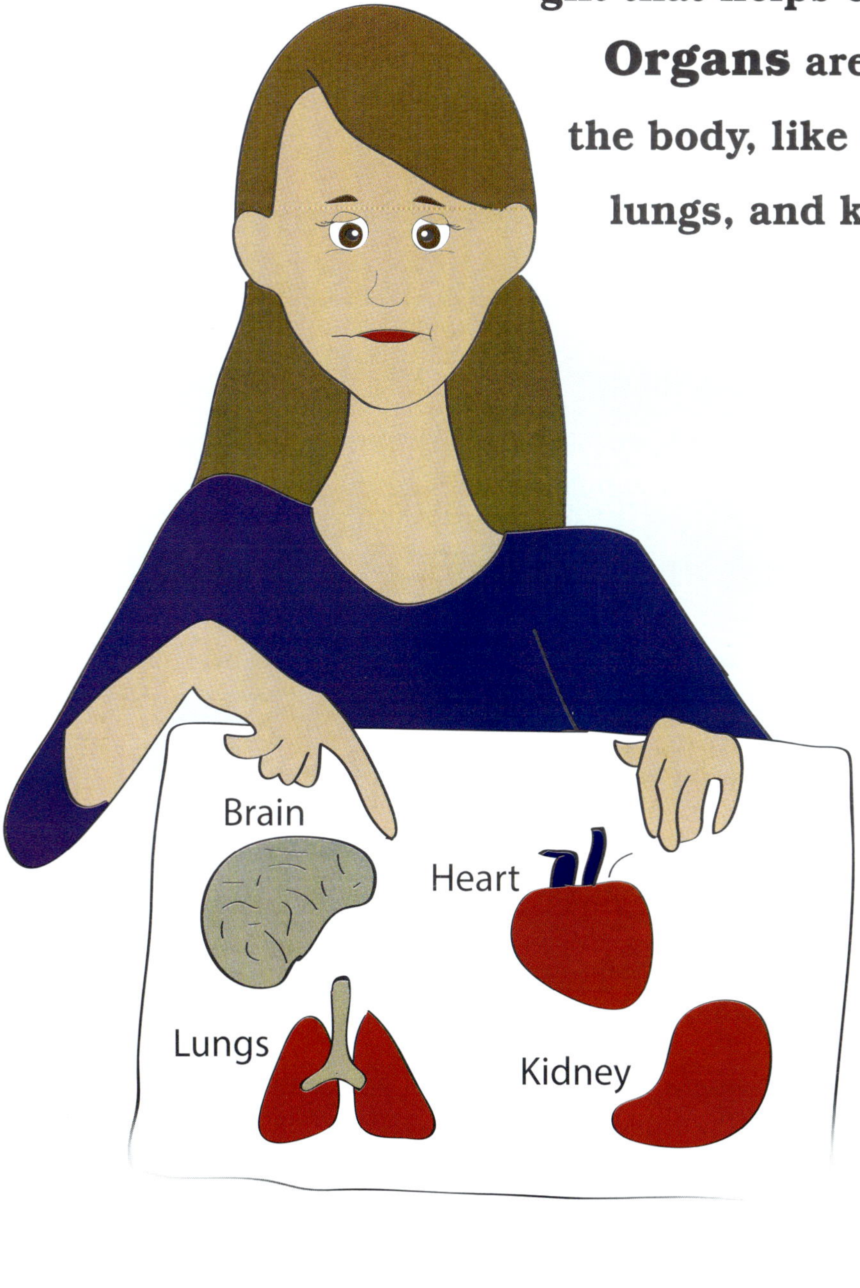

"Sometimes when someone's brain is hurt but the rest of the body is okay, doctors can take parts of the body, called organs, or tissue in the body, and give them to other people who are very sick. This is called organ or tissue donation."

"But how does that work?" Julian questioned, squeezing Boo tightly.

"Special doctors remove parts of the body and put them into the bodies of other people who need them," his mom answered.

"Doesn't that hurt?" Julian asked.

"No, remember, I told you your daddy's brain was not working, so he couldn't feel anything."

“How did they get them out?” Julian asked.

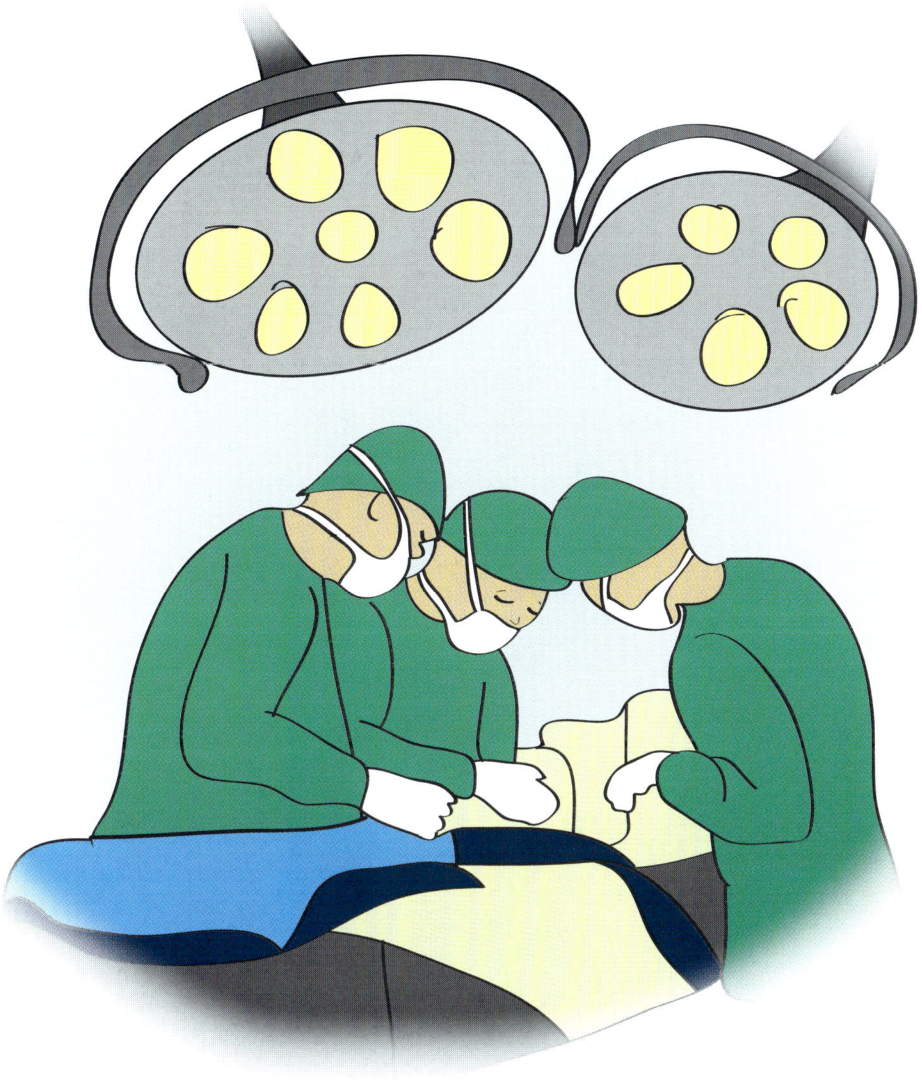

“The doctors do surgery. That means they make a cut on the body and take out the organs very carefully, so they can be put into the bodies of someone else to save their lives.”

"This is a very special gift. It is the gift of life. Giving this gift makes your daddy a hero."

"We are very sad that he is not with us, but we know he would be proud that he helped save other people through his death, just like he helped other people when he was here with us."

Although he was still very sad, Julian felt warm and fuzzy in his heart, as he hugged Boo, knowing that his dad gave the most special gift, the gift of life. His daddy was a hero.